The Literary Heritage of Holderness

I0098176

Phil Mathison

Published by Dead Good Publications
Newport,
East Yorkshire
HU15 2RF

© 2023

Other titles by the author

The Dead Good DADGAD Book
(ISBN 9780954693701)
The Dead Good Wacky Chord Book
(ISBN 9780954693725)
Shed Bashing with The Beatles
(ISBN 9780954693732)
The Spurn Gravel Trade
(ISBN 9780954693763)
Edited by: Captain Arthur Mathison - Now the long trick's over
(ISBN 9780954693770)
The Saint of Spurn Point
(ISBN 9780956299406)
Tolkien in East Yorkshire 1917 - 1918
(ISBN 9780956299413)
On Macabre Lines
(ISBN 9780956299420)
The Legendary Lost Town of Ravenser
(ISBN 9780956299437)
All Washed Up
(ISBN 9780956299444)
Sails, Paddles and Rails
(ISBN 9780956299451)

ISBN 978-0-9562994-6-8

Published by Dead Good Publications
Newport,
East Yorkshire
HU15 2RF

Contents

Foreword

The idea for this small volume on the literary connections of Holderness began about twenty years ago, when I picked up on the Tolkien strand. Through my research I then encountered other authors who I felt deserved some recognition in the due fullness of time.

What is included within the pages of this publication are writers of fiction who were either born in Holderness, had family roots here, or wrote about places within this ancient Yorkshire wapentake. I have not included authors who are alive today, such as Val Wood, Robert Edric, Penny Grubb, Tom Wells etc. All the writers noted within the pages of this book have passed away, for the most modern entry is Paul Bourquin, who died in 2009. So my subjects are writers of previous centuries, starting with Geoffrey Chaucer in the 14th century.

There have been a number of authors of non-fiction with Holderness connections, and once again, these creative people are outside the remit of this work. Therefore, such notable volumes as George Poulson's 'The History of the Seignority of Holderness' or Thomas Thompson's 'Ocellum Promontorium' and 'The History of the Church and Priory of Swine in Holderness' are also outside the scope of this publication.

I would like to acknowledge several people who have provided assistance with this book. First must be my wife, Mary, who lends a willing ear to my chosen topic of research, as well as being an excellent proof reader. Dr Jan Crowther has always been a fount of knowledge on the area, and willing to share any resources about Holderness that she feels will assist. Additionally, Jan has allowed me use of research undertaken by Peter, her deceased husband. Next I must mention Pat Moor, who through her love of family history, has been an enormous help to me in trawling the internet for censuses, electoral rolls, newspaper articles, genealogy etc. Without her research and input, this slim publication would have been even slimmer! My friend and local poet, Shane Blades, kindly unearthed information on Philip Larkin and Ted Hughes for me. Naturally, the Hull History Centre and the Beverley Treasure House have likewise proved invaluable at various stages of my research. Various internet sources have been used for additional material in this collection of 'mini biographies'.

If I have failed to credit any of my other assistants, trust me, any help with my research, no matter how small, has been appreciated. I hope that the end result presented here is some small recompense for any input I have received from many people over the years.

Andrew Marvell

We start our literary tour with one of the most famous sons of
Holderness. Andrew Marvell was born on March 31st 1621 in the
village of Winestead, near Patrington. His father, who originally was
from Cambridgeshire, was also called Andrew. He was a Church of
England clergyman, who upon ordination in 1608 had taken up the
living at Flamborough. He then moved to Winestead church,
dedicated to St. Germanus, in 1614, before relocating to the Holy
Trinity church in Hull as a preacher ten years later.

His wife, Anne, was a Yorkshire woman and bore him five children,
Anne, Mary, Elizabeth, Andrew and John. Sadly, John only lived for
one year, and was buried in the graveyard at Winestead in 1624.
Andrew junior, was educated at the Grammar School in Hull until
1633, when he entered Trinity College, Cambridge. He was to study
there until 1639, when he received a BA degree. The writer's first
poems were written in Greek and Latin and published while he was
still at Cambridge. He then began a career that included periods as
poet, private tutor, civil servant, satirist, pamphleteer and politician.
Unfortunately, the great man lost his mother in 1638, and his father,
who had remarried, was drowned in the Humber in 1641.

So at the age of only 20, Andrew Marvell had to navigate the
treacherous waters of English politics in the 1640s without his
parents' guidance. By instinct, he was a moderate royalist and an
Anglican, having briefly flirted with Catholicism. He travelled much
of Europe in these years, and it has been suggested that he was
appointed as a tutor to an aristocrat while on this 'Grand Tour'. He
visited Rome in 1645, and managed to avoid most of the civil war by
being away on the continent. It is alleged that during this sojourn the
poet mastered four languages, including Italian, French and Spanish.

Settling in London at the end of the decade, he became a moderate
parliamentarian as Cromwell rose to power. Despite writing a poem

called 'Horatian Ode' about sadness at the execution of Charles the first, he managed to steer a steady course through the turbulent politics of the time by also praising Oliver Cromwell on his return from Ireland.

Around the year 1650, he was appointed the private tutor in foreign languages to the daughter of Lord Thomas Fairfax at Nun Appleton Hall, situated between Selby and York. Fairfax was also a writer and encouraged Marvell. It was during this stay in his native Yorkshire that he wrote the poem 'Upon Appleton, to My Lord Fairfax', describing the estate, and also his best known work 'To His Coy Mistress'. In fact, much of the poet's output was written whilst there, and he produced little poetry after he left the hall in 1653. The focus of his life from then on moved towards establishing himself as a satirist and the world of politics called. During the years 1649 to 1660, historically defined as 'The Commonwealth', he became a friend and colleague of John Milton.

One of his early works of satire was 'Character of Holland', written during the First Anglo-Dutch War in 1652. After becoming a tutor to William Dutton at Eton in 1653, he moved on to be an assistant in the office of the foreign secretary in 1657. Again, Marvell wrote poems praising Cromwell at this time. In 1658, Marvell was elected as one of the MPs for Kingston upon Hull in the Third Protectorate Parliament. He held the seat, apart from a short period, until his death.

After the monarchy was restored in 1660, Marvell managed to avoid punishment for his co-operation with Cromwell, and was even able to convince King Charles II not to execute his friend John Milton. The writer then went on to write a number of bitterly satirical verses about corruption at the court, published anonymously to protect his good name and safety. Not until well after his demise was he identified as the author. More satire followed during the Second Anglo-Dutch War later that decade; political corruption, as always, being the focal point of his ire.

From 1659 until his passing, Marvell served as the London agent for the Hull Trinity House Shipmasters' Guild. As the secretary to the Embassy of the Earl of Carlisle, he undertook two missions to the continent, one to Russia, Germany, Denmark and Sweden. The other mission was to the Dutch Republic.

A number of satirical works followed in the 1670s, the first being an attack on Samuel Parker in 1672. Entitled 'The Rehearsal Transposed', it appeared in two parts, one in 1672, followed by the second part the next year. By this time he was a conforming Anglican, and was opposed to episcopacy. Marvell identified himself as being a Protestant, but not a Puritan. A keen parliamentarian, he was widely acknowledged as a man of incorruptible integrity. In later life he lived on Highgate Hill in North London, and there is now a bronze plaque to commemorate this.

He died suddenly on August 16th 1678, while in Hull attending a meeting of some of his old constituents. As his health had hitherto been good, some suspected that he had been poisoned by his clerical or political enemies. The great man was buried in central London, at the church of St Giles in the Fields.

His literary work would not have come to light but for the greed of his landlady, Mary Palmer. Claiming to be his wife (Marvell never married), she published his poems under the title 'Miscellaneous Poems of Andrew Marvell' in 1681. She alleged that there had been a secret marriage in 1667. This volume introduced such fine poems as 'To His Coy Mistress' to the world, and helped ultimately to establish him as one of Britain's finest poets.

Portrait of Andrew Marvell

Winestead church, which was the parish of Andrew Marvell's father

Sarah Stickney Ellis

The name of Stickney is historically closely linked with the hall called Ridgemont, just east of Burstwick in the district of Skeckling. William Stickney, who was born on September 20th 1764 at Beverley, married Esther Richardson of Ayton on September 22nd 1788 at a Quaker ceremony at Guisborough in the North Riding.

Sarah Stickney, their fifth child, was born to them in Burstwick on February 2nd 1799, and was brought up as a Quaker, but in later life moved to being Independent or Congregationalist in her religious convictions. Her mother died at Owstwick on March 18th 1803, when she was only four and this affected her for the rest of her life. William, her father, remarried in 1808, and went on to have four more children. Sarah did attend school, but was largely educated at home, and also helped raise the younger half-siblings. However, with the agricultural depression that set in during the 1820s affecting her father's finances, she had to find some way to earn a living. Initially, she painted portraits and undertook some drawing, but when these avenues failed to provide enough income, she turned her hand to writing. Her first work was on a sensitive subject - 'The Negro Slave: A Tale Addressed to the Women of Great Britain'. This title must have generated some income, as she then went on to write almost a book a year until her demise.

Recognition as an author came with her writings in the publications of 'Pictures of Private Life' (1833-1837) and 'The Poetry of Life' (1835). At this time, her work did not show much originality, but it did garner some praise. Additionally, she contributed to 'The Christian Keepsake and Missionary Annual'. This was edited by a widower, Rev William Ellis, whose wife, Mary Mercy Moor, had died in 1835. The recently bereaved William met Sarah at the home of a mutual friend who held a position at the London Missionary Society, of which Miss Stickney was a member.

Born in London on the 29th of August 1794, Rev Ellis was to marry Sarah at her home village, Burstwick, on May 23rd 1837. On the same occasion, she officially converted to Congregationalism. By the time of their marriage, Sarah was already an established writer. Unfortunately, they were unable to enjoy a honeymoon, for William's eldest daughter, Mary, was ill, and subsequently died in June. Apart from their shared love of books (he also went on to write several books), they had a common interest in missionary work and the cause of temperance. Sarah now had an instant family, as William had four children. Mary died shortly after the marriage, but she became close to the remaining three, Elizabeth, Annie and John. The two girls were to be educated at the school that Sarah had established, along with a friend, in Hoddesdon, Hertfordshire, called Rawdon House. It appears that the couple had one child of their own, William George, born in Rothwell in 1838. In the 1851 census, William lived at East Ardsley, near Leeds, and he married in 1867. The two girls eventually went on to teach at Rawdon House. Unfortunately, the ladies were not to reach a great age, for Elizabeth died in 1858 and Annie in 1862.

William had already had some success as an author, writing about the ethnography of Polynesia after living and working there for the London Missionary Society between 1816 and 1824. . He also wrote about topography, history and botany and was supportive of his wife's burgeoning literary career, which took up increasing amounts of her time. He knew that he had married an independently minded woman.

Examining her writing, Sarah proved successful at chronicling women's roles within society. Her best known titles are works on how ladies should conduct themselves - 'The Women of England', published in 1839, followed by 'The Daughters of England' in 1842, and in 1843 two titles in one year - 'The Wives of England' and 'The Mothers of England'. They proved extremely popular and received reviews in many journals across England and America. These included 'The Christian Remembrancer'; 'Tait's Edinburgh Magazine'; 'The Church of England Quarterly Review'; 'The Athenaeum'; 'The Congregational Magazine'; 'The American Biblical Repository'; 'The Eclectic Review'; 'Meliora', and 'The Southern Quarterly Review', plus 'The Quarterly Review'. William Makepeace Thackeray even poked fun at her works, showing how widely read her books had become in the 1840s. It has even been suggested that Emily Bronte chose her pseudonym 'Ellis Bell' because of Sarah Ellis's standing in the culture of the time. Her father passed away in 1848 in Holderness.

The author also turned her attention to a subject close to her heart, education, and wrote the titles 'Rawdon House' (about her school) and in 1869, 'Education of the Heart: Women's Best Work'. The Ellises lived at Hoddesdon from 1841 until their deaths, and founded a local temperance association in that town. The school was non-denominational, unusual at the time, and was intended to inculcate the principle of "moral training, the formation of character, and in some degree the domestic duties of young ladies." She stressed the significance of women receiving an intellectual education as well as those skills necessary for domestic duties. Naturally, there was a strong emphasis on moral character when raising children.

Although Sarah was a child of her time, in that women should know their place and accept their domestic role, there was another aspect to her commentary. She believed that ladies were best not to marry if they could not find a reasonable husband. In private correspondence, she relates stories of friends experiencing disharmony in their middle-class marriages, and in fact her own experience of marriage may have also tempered her comments. Additionally, she had no qualms about instructing wives to manipulate their husbands for the sake of marital harmony and to also achieve their own ends.

After 35 years of marriage, Sarah and William died within a week of each other. Her death was on June 16th 1872. Now largely forgotten, it is hard to imagine that by the time of her death, Sarah had published over forty books, and was well known in both the U.K. and America. Of independent mind, she was buried in the countryside near their home, whilst her husband was laid to rest in the Congregationalists' non-denominational Abney Park Cemetery on the outskirts of Victorian London.

Portrait of Sarah Stickney Ellis

Ridgemont Hall, where Sarah Stickney Ellis was born in 1799

Mary Elizabeth Braddon

The famous Victorian author was born on October 4th 1835 in Soho, London. To appear younger, she often stated that her date of birth was 1837. She was the third child of Fanny, (nee White) Braddon and Henry Braddon. Her parents separated in 1840 due to her father's infidelities, which at the time was very unconventional. Mary had two siblings, Maggie, who was eleven years her elder and Edward, older by six years.

She was privately educated, attending Scarsdale and then Dartmouth Lodge boarding school. From an early age she was keen on writing, having been given a writing desk by her godfather. Her brother, Edward, left for India and then Australia when she was just ten.

Upon leaving school, she moved to Bath and started acting. Mary hoped to be able to support her mother, since trying to keep up appearances after the departure of Henry must have been a struggle. In 1852 she commenced her career as an actress, but was forced to adopt a stage name – Mary Seyton, to avoid controversy for her family, who disagreed with her choice of profession. She toured, initially visiting Southampton, Winchester, and Reading and even reached Scotland. Most of the productions that she appeared in were either comedies or farces, but she also tackled pantomime, burlesques and even Shakespeare. Initially, she was just an extra or had supporting roles, but had moved on to lead roles by 1856. It was in that year that she settled in Surrey so that she could launch her career in London. However, some of her reviews were not favourable and her first season in the capital was not a success. Therefore, she looked to the provinces once more.

By the end of 1856, Mary was to be found in Beverley, for she had joined the company of Messrs. Wolfenden and Melbourne in the Queen's Theatre, Hull, and performed six nights at the Beverley Assembly Rooms. The actress also stayed with a family in Hull living on Smeaton Street at that time.

She was soon on the move again, this time to Brighton in 1857, to join Henry Nye Chart's company. However, the roles that she now got were less suitable for her, suggesting that her popularity was waning. Realising that an actress's career was destined to be short-lived, she turned her hand to writing. By this time, through her stage work, she had become known to Edward Bulwer Lytton, who, along with John Gilby, encouraged her pursuit of writing as a profession. Indeed, in 1860, her comedietta, 'The loves of Arcadia', was produced at the Strand Theatre.

Braddon returned to Beverley again in 1859, spending six months as governess at Black House Farm, Beverley Parks. By this date she had given up acting. It was while residing here for the second time that the seeds of her future career were sown. She had already had articles published fairly regularly in a Brighton newspaper, helped by a young man called William Sawyer. However, in the East Riding market town, she set about a double literary project. A local printer, C R Empson, of Toll Gavel, commissioned a sensational serial, called 'Three Times Dead', which appeared in 1860. The work later re-appeared as 'The Trial of the Serpent'. The novel was not a success, but gave the writer some insight into the publishing industry. Additionally, a local patron, a certain John Gilby mentioned above, requested a book of poems about Garibaldi, entitled 'Garibaldi and Other Poems'. It was published in 1861. Using her stage name, Mary also had her book of poems published in 'The Beverley Recorder & General Advertiser'. It was during this six month stay that Braddon probably visited Withernsea, a town that was to surface in her novel 'Lady Audley's Secret', renamed as 'Wildernsea'.

At the very beginning of the 1860s, Mary met John Maxwell, an Irishman born in 1824, who was trying to make his way in the competitive world of London magazine publishing. They became lovers, but behaved as if they were married. The truth was even stranger, for Maxwell actually had a wife, Mary Ann Crowley, who by then resided with her family. He already had five children by her, and she lived until 1874, after which Mary and John formally married at St Bride's Church in Fleet Street, London, on October 2nd of that year.

However, John Maxwell was constantly in financial distress, and to help him out, Mary set about writing what would become her blockbuster 'Lady Audley's Secret'. The work appeared in October 1862, under the name M E Braddon, which was gender neutral, and ran to no less than eight editions before the end of that year. The book transformed her prospects, and from then on she went on to be the author of at least eighty books, with another successful novel, 'Aurora Floyd' following in 1863.

A considerable quantity of her work was published anonymously, for she had a prodigious work rate, and often produced work at short notice. However, to her life's end, 'Lady Audley's Secret' was always her favourite, and never went out of print during her lifetime. Braddon's work could be broadly described as crime, mystery and detection, but she moved away from criminal plotlines after about 1890. By this time, Mary had ultimately established herself not only in society, but had also found critical acclaim as an author of substance.

We can see that the writer's own unconventional adult life reflected her upbringing, with parents who had separated. Victorian views on morality were very strict, and it is perhaps because of her own personal experiences that Braddon went on to make her name as a sensational writer. Mary had six children to Maxwell – Gerald, Fanny, Francis, who unfortunately died at the tender age of three, William Babington, Winifred Rosalie and finally Edward Henry Harrington. Until they married they lived as common law husband and wife, so Mary endured ostracism not only for her sensational writing but also for her immoral life style. To subdue public gossip, Maxwell in 1864 stated that they were in fact married, but the truth came out when Richard Brinsley Knowles stated that his sister in law, Mary Ann, legal wife to Maxwell, was in fact still living! Despite the constant scandal all through the 1860s and into the 1870s, Mary and John settled down and moved to Chelsea, and the gossip gradually subsided.

After the failure of Maxwell's publication 'Robin Goodfellow', he went on to produce another journal called 'The Sixpenny Magazine', but after 1866, Mary founded her own magazines, 'Belgravia' and 'The Belgravia Annual'. As for her novels, up until 1871, Ward Lock had published her titles. Maxwell then published her output until 1888, when Simpkin, Marshall & Co took over responsibility for her books. Braddon sold 'Belgravia' and 'The Belgravia Annual' in 1878 and Maxwell then started 'The Mistletoe Bough', a Christmas fiction annual.

In later life, her works were often adapted for the stage, sometimes without her permission. Ultimately, 'Lady Audley's Secret' went on to be adapted for television and film. Although her health had begun to deteriorate, Mary not only moved house a number of times, but even bought a car in 1912! She attended the cinematic release of 'Aurora Floyd' in 1913, and in 1914 helped with the war effort by performing charitable work with hospital patients. The writer died on February 4th 1915 in Richmond and is interred in the cemetery there. Her home in the centre of town, Lichfield House, is now listed.

I leave you with the description in chapter 27 of 'Lady Audley's Secret' of the protagonist's journey to the thinly disguised resort of Withernsea.

"Within an hour of the receipt of this message, Mr. Audley arrived at the King's-Cross station, and took his ticket for Wildernsea by an express train that started at a quarter before two.
The shrieking engine bore him on the dreary northward journey, whirling him over desert wastes of flat meadow-land and bare cornfields, faintly tinted with fresh sprouting green. This northern

road was strange and unfamiliar to the young barrister, and the wide expanse of the wintry landscape chilled him by its aspect of bare loneliness. The knowledge of the purpose of his journey blighted every object upon which his absent glances fixed themselves for a moment, only to wander wearily away; only to turn inward upon that far darker picture always presenting itself to his anxious mind.

It was dark when the train reached the Hull terminus, but Mr. Audley's journey was not ended. Amidst a crowd of porters and scattered heaps of that incongruous and heterogeneous luggage with which travellers incumber themselves, he was led, bewildered and half asleep, to another train which was to convey him along the branch line that swept past Wildernsea, and skirted the border of the German Ocean.

Half an hour after leaving Hull, Robert felt the briny freshness of the sea upon the breeze that blew in at the open window of the carriage, and an hour afterward the train stopped at a melancholy station, built amid a sandy desert, and inhabited by two or three gloomy officials, one of whom rung a terrific peal upon a harshly clanging bell as the train approached."

Portrait of Mary Elizabeth Braddon in her younger days

WITHERNSEA, A NEW WATERING PLACE ON THE EAST COAST.

Withernsea as a resort in Braddon's day. Note the station on the right

Sarah Grand

Frances Elizabeth Bellenden Clarke was to become one of the most famous women writers of the late Victorian and Edwardian period, but to her many readers, she was by then known as Sarah Grand. Her parents were Edward John Bellenden Clarke, who was born in England on October 26th 1813 and Margaret Bell Sherwood, whose nativity was the same year. Margaret's roots were at Rysome Garth, near Holmpton, hence the Holderness connection.

Looking at the family's Holderness connections, we discover that in the 1851 Census, the residents of Rysome Garth were George Henry Sherwood, then aged 69, and his wife, Margaret Sherwood (nee Bell), aged 68. They lived with their unmarried son William, who had been born at Rysome Garth, and is noted as being 36 years of age. It appears that George, who had come from Skeffling, farmed no less than 543 acres of land, and employed thirteen labourers.

George passed away on February 2nd 1854, and so by the time of the 1861 Census, William, now a married man was the head of the household at Rysome Garth. However, he only employed six men and one boy on the same acreage. William was still there when they undertook the 1871 Census, employing five men and now six boys. His wife, Mary Ann(e) Charlotte Sherwood (nee Boynton) is now recorded at this location. Her father was Henry Boynton Baronet of Burton Agnes, so they were well connected to county society. However, by the time of the 1889 Kelly's Directory, James Blashill was now the listed farmer at Rysome. This ended a very long connection with the place. Bulmers Directory of 1892 states that 'Rysome Garth, a manor and estate of 543 acres belonged to the Sherwoods for about a century'. Additionally 'The County Families of the UK 1864' states that The Sherwood family even then had been associated with Rysome Garth for four generations.

Returning to Frances's parents, they had married at St. Andrew,

Holborn in London on March 24th 1840, so it is reasonable to assume that Margaret had left her family home in Rysome by that time. Serving as a naval coast officer, Edward was posted to Ireland in 1852. In the year 1854, the Clarke family were residing at Rosebank House, Donaghadee in County Down, and that is where Frances Elizabeth was born on June 10th 1854.

When her father died in Mayo, Ireland on May 6th 1862, Margaret, described as 'impoverished' in an article of the time, wished to return to the county of her birth. Therefore, she moved back to the East Riding of Yorkshire to be near her folks. 5 Prospect Street, Bridlington Quay was to be the family's home, and as far as I am aware, Frances was to live in Bridlington until her marriage in 1870. Her mother died not long afterwards, on November 27th 1874. Frances's education seems to have been sporadic. Indeed, she was expelled from the Royal Naval School in Twickenham in 1868 for orchestrating groups to protest at the 'Contagious Diseases Act', an act designed to persecute prostitutes and subject them to the indignity of intimate inspections and be confined in hospital wards. She was sent then to a finishing school in Kensington, and while in London, met David Chambers McFall, who was considerably her senior and already with two sons from a previous marriage.

Frances Elizabeth married McFall in August 1870, when she was only sixteen years of age. At the time of the 1871 Census, they are noted as living at Shorncliffe House, Cheriton, Eltham, Kent. David had been born in 1833 in India, and the 1881 Census described him as a general surgeon. The couple then had a child of their own, David Archibald Edward, who was born on October 7th 1871. The family then traveled extensively in the Far East, which informed much of her later writing. They initially resided in Norwich upon their return to England, but by 1881, the family had moved to 15 Folly Lane, Warrington, Cheshire, for David had retired.

By then, the marriage had become strained, and Frances turned to writing to express herself. Her first novel 'Ideala' was self published in 1888, but achieved little success. Undeterred, she decided in 1890 to leave her husband and move to London to further her career, for a recent law enabled her to retain her personal property and this decision encouraged her. Having married an army surgeon, she was familiar with sexually transmitted diseases, and used this knowledge to advantage in her 1893 work 'The Heavenly Twins', which was published by Heinemann.

By the time of its publication, Clarke had restyled herself as Sarah Grand. Her new pen name was a statement on her feminist stand, and what, in a debate with Ouida, she described in 1894 as the ideal of 'The New Woman'. She was not totally anti-marriage, but felt that too many women were trapped in loveless unions and deplored the inequality of the system that reinforced this. The subject of suffocation for the wife within marriage is a consistent theme in her writing. Her writing encouraged women to work, learn and challenge the limitations of conventional marriage. She believed in political action and that middle-class women had a duty to speak out and help to mould the future of the nation.

In 1894, the novel 'Our Manifold Nature' was published, followed by 'The Beth Book' in 1897, which contained some autobiographical detail.

After her husband's death in February 1898, Grand moved to Tunbridge Wells, Kent. She became active in local women's suffrage societies, and her stepson illustrator and writer, Haldane MacFall, lodged with her for several years. The publication of 'The Heavenly Twins' made her famous, and she traveled a great deal, particularly to the U.S.A.. The notoriety of the book made her open to much criticism, but others, like George Bernard Shaw, applauded her work.

Moving to Crowe Hall, Widcombe, Bath in 1920, she became more engaged with politics than with writing. Indeed, her last work was 'Variety', which came out in 1922. She served as Mayoress of Bath between 1922 and 1929 alongside Mayor Cedric Chivers. When her home was bombed during 1942, she made the decision to move to Calne in Wiltshire, where she died on May 12th the following year. Her son, Archie was to outlive her by only a year, for he died in an air raid on London in 1944. She is interred in the Lansdown Cemetery in Bath, Somerset.

Portrait of Sarah Grand at the time of her fame

Sarah's mother came from Rysome Garth near Holmpton

Flit & Ko

Earlier in the book, mention was made of Mrs Sarah Stickney Ellis, born at Ridgemont, Burstwick. Her family were Quakers, and as such there was a close link with the Foster family of Hilston, who also shared that religious persuasion. This area of Holderness was rather a Quaker stronghold, there being a meeting house in Owstwick, acquired in 1670. In fact, William Stickney was the last person buried there, on July 9th 1848. After 1850, friends met at a building adjacent to Stickney's farm.

It is with the Foster family at Hilston that we now continue our exploration of literature in Holderness, for both Florence Elizabeth Foster and Catherine Storr Foster were to achieve local fame in the closing years of the 19th century. Catherine was born on September 23rd 1864, with Florence's birth being noted as January 5th 1869, though some sources suggest the year 1867.

They were the daughters of William Foster, born December 4th 1808 in Manchester, and Hannah Stickney, born at Burton Pidsea on the 5th of July, 1829. William Foster was recorded at the time as being a Clergyman and landowner. Their maternal grandparents were Joseph Stickney (1792 - 1866), a farmer of Burton Pidsea, and Eliza Mennell, and their paternal grandparents were Jonathan Foster and Mary Storr, and this is almost certainly where Catherine's middle name originates from. Interestingly there's an octagonal tower in Hilston known as Admiral Storr's Tower, built in 1750 as a lookout for Joseph Storr, a member of another Quaker family. He died not long after in 1753. From the probate records, we discover that William Foster and Hannah were married in Edinburgh on the 18th September 1860.

William Foster died in 1880, leaving 109 acres to his son, W H Foster, who passed away in 1900. Hannah stayed on in Hilston for a while, but by 1901, the census of that year shows her as residing in

Burton Pidsea. Some time in the final decade of the 19th century, the Foster girls started writing, and in the case of Catherine, also illustrating. It would appear that the local publishers, Brown & Sons of Hull took an interest in their work, publishing the title 'Reel No 8 and Suddaby Fewster, Two Holderness Tales' at the start of the 1890s. The book was illustrated by J Walter West (and others). Could the 'other' have been Catherine's first published example of illustrating? The stories are about fictional characters typical of the Holderness villages that the sisters would know so well. There is a dedication in the front of 'Reel No 8' to Sophia Helena Stickney "Many happy hours in Holderness". We see here how strong the Foster / Stickney connection is. Incidentally, Sophia, born in 1853, died in 1939 and is buried in New Walk Cemetery in Beverley.

Their next title was 'How to be happy though hunted, from the Foxes' Point of View', published by Brown & Sons of Hull again, almost certainly in 1896. This title was well received, as it ran to a second edition, also published by Browns. The preliminaries to the book contains the following warm dedication - 'To Captain W H Foster, A.S.C., with best wishes for the 12th November, this story is most affectionately dedicated by Flit'. They also note that Flit is Miss Foster of 'The Cottage' Hilston, near Hull. As mentioned above, Captain Foster was in charge of the estate in the closing years of Victoria's reign. The narrative concerns foxes from all over South Holderness meeting at Humbleton Sticks to discuss the ethics of hunting. The tale mentions the mild winter of 1895 / 1896 with few frosty days. The significance of this is that there had been greater opportunity for hunting! Some of the other local places mentioned are Hatfield, Halsham-Whins, Danthorpe, Humbleton and Owstwick. To discover the outcome of this unusual and heated debate, you will have to read the book yourself! The title was even resurrected by the Malet Lambert Local History Society in 1984 and re-issued as Extra Volume No 76.

'A Holderness Harvest', with 'Flit' as the author, was published by Brown & Sons in the closing years of the 19th century. Florence E

Foster is listed as the illustrator. As part of promotion for the new book, the publisher mentions the previous titles "How to be happy though hunted, from the Foxes' Point of View' and notes that she is the joint author of Reel No 8'. At one point, the story refers to the newly built Withernsea Lighthouse.

The next novel to appear was a bit of a departure. Entitled 'The Goblin', it is the story of Archie Luttrell, so nick-named by his father. For a change, the book was published in London by Wells, Gardner, Darton & Co. in 1900. The preliminaries of the publication list the three previous titles by the sisters, even though the profits of the sales would go to the Hull publisher. As the reader follows the tale of young Archie, we meet Mrs Dibnah, wife of a sporting farmer who resides at Kilnsea. The narrative also includes the characters of Calliard, the Norseby family, and Lord Fenshire, who had all been mentioned in 'A Holderness Harvest'. Archie spends time at Spurn and even the Outer Binks off the Point are chronicled.

By the time of the 1901 census, Hannah, their mother, recorded as a widow, lived at Burton Pidsea, with Catherine still noted as residing at Hilston. Beyond this date, no further books from the Foster sisters have been brought to my attention. However, interestingly, the Berwickshire Gazette of 22nd of May, 1906 includes a short story entitled 'The Toy Hospital' and the tale is credited to Catherine S Foster. Are there other stories by the Fosters hiding in the pages of similar provincial newspapers and magazines of the Edwardian age one wonders? However, what we do know is that Hannah, still residing at Burton Pidsea, passed away on March 11th 1909.

At some time the sisters must have moved away, for Catherine is listed as residing at 'Lairgate', White Rose Lane, Woking and was noted in the 1931 census as being of private means. This location was still her recorded place of residence when she died, aged 81 years, at Roseacre Nursing Home, Priorsfield Road, Compton, Surrey, on February 15th 1946. Florence, also resident at that address, lived even longer, finally passing away on July 20th 1959 at Park

Bungalow, Burleigh, Minchinhampton, Gloucestershire. By then, she was at least 92 years old. So ended the era of charming tales from a noted family whose Holderness roots went back well over a century.

Hilston cottage, where Florence and Catherine Foster were born

The cover of Catherine & Florence Foster's 1900 book 'The Goblin'

Harry A Spurr

This next author we look at was a chance find by me during the lockdown in 2020. I ordered a copy of 'Holmpton; A Journey Through Time' by P A Leckonby & H M Hall. There on page 105 was the name Harry A Spurr and mention of his novel 'A Cockney in Arcadia', published in 1899! Having spent many years on the trail of local authors, this was a bolt from the blue.

Harry was born in Sculcoates, Hull, in late 1869 to Thomas and Mary Spurr. Thomas was born in Rothwell, Leeds c1829. By 1851 he had moved to 144 Finkle Street, Selby, and worked as an attorney's general clerk and confectioner. He met Mary Burton, a native of the town, and they married. Their first child was Thomas William, and Melanchthon Burton Spurr soon followed, being born in Selby on 1 March 1852. They obviously then moved south, for their third child, Martha Elizabeth, was born in Harwich in 1856. However by 1860, the family had taken residence in Hull.

By 1861 the couple resided at 12 Percy Street in Hull and Thomas was listed in the directories of the day as being occupied as an attorney and solicitor. Letitia Spurr was born in July 1861, and her birth is registered as being in Sculcoates.

Thomas had left Percy Street by 1863 and lived at 5 Kingston Square, which was the registered address of Spurr & Richardson. Apparently they also had premises at Bank Buildings, 11 Scale Lane, registered as solicitors, and they were agents for Gresham Life Office. Thomas was still in the legal profession in 1892, for the trade directories list him as a solicitor and commissioner of oaths, operating from 56 Lowgate. His partner, Richardson, is not mentioned after 1878, so one assumes that he had left the concern.

Harry was born in late 1869 and was also registered as being in the parish of Sculcoates. In 1871, when he was just one year old, the family moved once again, this time to Eldon Grove, Beverley Road, Hull. His formative years were spent at a residence with the grandiose title of Chandros Villa Theatre Royal, Beverley Road, Hull and this was to be the family home until 1889, by which time he was twenty years of age.

The young H A Spurr became interested in the theatre and also journalism. In 1891 the writer is recorded as living at Cardross House, Cottingham, probably with his parents, as the Hull directories of 1892 have this as their home address. His occupation is listed as a journalist (author) and sub-editor. This work was probably with regard to 'The Hull Quiz:' a local weekly satirical paper, for in 1895, he is noted as the editor of this publication. It was in this magazine, between January 12th and May 25th of that year that he published 'Bachelor Ballads'.

Harry Astley Spurr married Harriet 'Hetty' Loftus on June 15th, 1895 at Park Street Church in Hull. Harriet was born in 1871 in Leeds, and outlived all members of the Spurr family, for she did not die until 5th September 1953 and by that time was living at 66 Sunnybank, Hull. However, after the marriage, the couple must have had wanderlust, because soon afterwards they were living in London.

Whether they quickly tired of the capital or for whatever reason, they had moved back to Yorkshire and made Holmpton, near Withernsea their home in 1896. It was here that Harry, resident at Park Lodge, wrote the novel 'A Cockney in Arcadia', in which it would appear that many of the characters in the book were based on local figures. The book was illustrated by the well known artist John Hassall, and was published by George Allen & Unwin. He and his wife spent three years living in the village (which in the book he calls 'Hometown') until 1899, before returning to London. Humorously, he calls Hull in the book 'Dulltown', in contrast to his affectionate renaming of Holmpton as 'Hometown'. One autobiographical detail in the novel is the reference to living near Kings Cross, which the author did during his time in London, circa 1895.

The fact that he considered himself a Cockney, even though he was a Yorkshireman who had spent such a short time in London, is rather comical. Prior to this date, his only published work was 'If we only knew, and other poems', co-written with his brother Mel B and produced by W Andrews & Co of Hull in 1893, and 'Bachelor Ballads' of 1895. His wife must have had a literary bent as well, for 'The Hull Times' published a story by Hett Spurr called 'The House by the Sea', with Withernsea as its backdrop in 1896.

By 1901, Harry and Harriet had moved back to London, for their home is recorded as being 14 Sainfoin Road, Streatham. By now, Harry is listed as being an author.

When researching Harry, I became confused by references to a certain Harry Spurr in connection with the well known supernatural writer, Arthur Machen. Eventually I surmised that there were two Harry Spurrs, and this explained why the Hull Mr Spurr started adding Astley as his middle name in 1895. The other Harry Spurr was born in London in 1860, and became the manager at George Redway's publishing business.

Harry A Spurr must have been an expert on Alexander Dumas, judging by the following three titles – 'Life and writings of Alexander Dumas', published by Dent in 1902; 'Stories from the plays of Alexander Dumas', published by Tutin in 1904, and 'Fairy Tales of Dumas' was then to follow. The last title was illustrated by Harry Rountree, and was published in the U.S.A. by Stokes in the year 1904.

Harry's parents, Thomas and Mary, had moved to 198 Park Avenue, Hull by 1902 and are recorded as living on their own. It was probably here that Thomas passed away in 1903, for the death is recorded as being in Sculcoates.

Melanchthon Burton Spurr, Harry's brother, went on to become a well known music hall artiste, having shown much potential as a musician when young. He also wrote many humorous ditties until he died when on tour in Australia in 1904. He was buried in St Kilda Cemetery, Melbourne on 25th Sept 1904. Harry wrote a book about him in 1905, called 'Mel B. Spurr: His life, work, writings and recitations', which was published by Browns of Hull. In the publication, Harry mentions their time together at Chandros Villa, and that Harry was often involved in Melanchthon's theatrical performances, such as 'Uncle's Will' and 'War to the Knife', with Miss Spurr also noted in the cast. Mel was also published in 'The Hull Quiz' mentioned above, for the January 26th issue contains his short story called 'The man of the hour'.

Harry was not to survive him very long, for on July 2nd 1906 he also died, in the seaside resort of Hornsea. However, his death is registered as being within the district of Skirlaugh. According to the obituary in the Hull Daily Mail the following day, he was to be buried at General Cemetery, Spring Bank, at 3.45 pm on that date. Unfortunately, his grave has not survived to the present day. The Spurrs were certainly not made of durable stock, for his brother Thomas William died young, and his sister, Letitia passed away in October the following year in Prestwich, Lancashire.

Park Lodge, where Harry A Spurr wrote 'A Cockney in Arcadia'

The title page of Harry's book about his time in Holmpton

Edward Charles Booth

Edward Charles Booth was born on November 11th 1872 to George and Mary Elizabeth, who lived at 39 Young Street, Doncaster. They had married in April 1867. He had two brothers, George Edward, who was born in 1868, and William Bromley, born in 1869. A sister, Alice Mary, had previously died after only living five days. The family moved to 44 Hall Gate in 1881, and Edward probably attended the private school on that street. It was a musical family, for his father was a professor of music, and played the organ at St. James Church, Doncaster. George was a pianist, but his brother, William, was the most distinguished musically, as well as being a talented artist. However, he chose to concentrate on music and became a violinist of considerable note. Edward selected the cello, and composed for this instrument. However, an accident to his bowing hand ended any chance of pursuing a professional career, although he continued to compose, the following two songs being of note - 'Mother England', published in 1905 which also included lyrics by him. The second song, 'To Fortune', with words by H Hammond – Spencer, followed in 1908, and was apparently a favourite of no less than Dame Clara Butt. It would appear that all three brothers taught music at some point in their careers. Edward also composed 'O Mistress Mine' for concerts, but as far as we know, this work was never published.

We know little of Edward's schooling, for he may have attended either Doncaster Grammar School or Hall Gate School, which educated his two brothers. By the time he was 17 years old, he had chance to stay at Oak Tree Farm in East Newton, near Aldbrough. He may have composed there, for there was a piano, but it is more likely that his talent for creative writing surfaced, for some details of this interlude appear in his novel 'The Cliff End'. This was the start of the author's connection with Holderness, for he also had holidays at a farm house at Out Newton, near Holmpton, and stayed at Laurel Farm, Skeffling. We must credit residence at these locations as giving

Edward local knowledge and an ear for the distinctive local dialect which he was to use to such advantage in later years.

His novels started being published in 1908, with the arrival of 'The Cliff End'. In the U.S.A., it was re-titled as 'The Post-Girl'. 1910 saw the appearance of 'The Doctor's Lass', followed by 'Fondie' in 1916 and 'The Tree of the Garden' after World War 1 in 1922. All these novels are set in Holderness, and make extensive use of dialect in the telling of the tales. The next book set in Holderness was 'Kith and Kin' in 1929, but this title had less local reference points. Apart from 'Kith and Kin' all his titles were published in the U.S.A. in the same year as his British editions. In fact, it was pressure from his American publishers that ensured that he continued writing his novels after 1922. The West Riding author, Phyllis Bentley, described E C Booth as 'The laureate of Holderness'. The Birmingham Post was even more effusive, stating in a revue for 'The Treble Clef' – "What Hardy is for Wessex, what George Eliot is to the Midlands, that is Mr Booth to the East Riding of Yorkshire".

Now let us look at some of the works and their relevance to Holderness. In 'The Cliff End', a young composer (perhaps based on himself?) arrives at Ullbrig, which would appear to be based on Aldbrough. One of the characters is Father Mostyn, reputed to have been a characterisation of Reverend Austin Price of St Bartholomew's church in the village. The book was an immediate success, being published by Grant Richards in 1908 and 1909, by J M Dent & Sons in the Wayfarers Library in 1914, and by T Fisher Unwin as a popular edition in 1924.

'The Doctor's Lass', published by Grant Richards in the U.K. in 1910 and in the U.S.A. by The Century Co, New York, also has some local markers, such as Sunfleet which appears to be either Skeffling or Welwick. There are bouts of drinking in Kenham beach, which is supposed to be Kilnsea. Patrington is renamed Peterwick, and Easington becomes Beachington. Spurn is also noted as Spraith!

Additionally, there is reference to the distant lights of Hull (Hunmouth) and Grimsby (Grimesthorpe).

The next book, 'Bella', was set in Scarborough, renamed as Spathorpe and was published by Edward Arnold in 1912, with a popular edition by T Fisher Unwin following in 1925. As the title is set outside Holderness, let us move on to 'Fondie', in which the author returns to our locality. Published in 1916 by Duckworth, it also appeared in America, courtesy of D Appleton & Co of New York. In this novel, Leven, or perhaps Withernwick appears in print as 'Whivvle'. Hornsea is imaginatively re-titled 'Meremsea', whereas Burton Constable becomes 'Mersham Hall'.

As mentioned above, it was his publishers in the States that encouraged him to write more, which rather prompts speculation as to why books featuring East Yorkshire dialect should be so popular in America. Therefore after a gap of several years, 'The Tree of the Garden' appeared. Published by Duckworth in 1922, the story follows a boy who holidays with a family called the Suddabys that farm in a place called Whinsett, which may be Dimlington. However, there is a Winsetts and a Whinsetts Road south of Skeffling. It is reputed that 'nearby Plumpton' is in fact Holmpton. Other places visited are Dimmlesea, which is Withernsea, Hunmouth which is again Hull, Spraith we have already met as Spurn and Hallum is surely a thinly disguised Hollym!

In 1924, T Fisher Unwin published 'Miss Parkworth and other stories'. This has no topographical references at all, as it is four short stories with little dialect, all set within an urban environment. In the same year, T Fisher Unwin published 'Treble Clef', an obvious musical reference used by Edward. In the U.S.A., the publishers Dodd Head & Co of New York did the honours. Again, this book is located outside our corner of Yorkshire, being set in Doncaster, which is renamed 'Daneborough'.

The final title relevant to Holderness is 'Kith and Kin', published by

Duckworth in 1929. There is mention of Hull Infirmary, and extensive use of dialect. No topography other than this is recorded, but there is an assumption that the background to the tale is Holderness, possibly set near Ottringham.

His last book was entitled 'The Brass Knocker' and was published by Jonathan Cape in the U.K. under the pseudonym of Edward Rathbone, and was a completely different type of tale. Though still set in a town, presumably Doncaster, it was a crime novel showing a dark side not previously seen in his work. Despite this departure in style, Edward still managed to find a publisher in New York, D Appleton Century.

Around the time of his first book, it is not clear where he or his brothers lived, but correspondence exists that is addressed to the Out Newton residence of Mrs. Douglas and Miss Maud Douglas, who probably was a child. It is known that Edward really liked this village on the edge of the Holderness cliffs. It should be noted that Edward may also have had intervals at Leeds, Doncaster and even Richmond in Surrey. However, in 1912, with his brother, William Bromley, he settled at Seaton House near Hornsea, which had been left to them by a cousin, Miss Sarah Emily Ward. It would appear that they were now undertaking considerably less musical touring, for William wrote in September 1914, just after the outbreak of the war, that they had both cancelled their final subscription concerts. A year later, while living at Seaton, Edward made his will.

The two brothers were well known locally, as they were both special constables, and continued to entertain people in the district with musical recitals. Edward was increasingly concentrating on his writing at this time, and indeed the high wall in their garden is mentioned in his book 'Fondie'. During World War 1, both brothers signed up to the Army Service Corps (now called the Royal Army Service Corps). Edward joined this division as a 2nd lieutenant on July 30th 1917. Their father had died in Ilkley in the January of the same year, at the age of eighty-six.

Edward moved to his final residence in 1926. Penistone Cottage, 3 The Park, Scalby was a large brick house that again had been left to them by cousin Miss Sarah Emily Ward. It appears that he shared the residence with George and William, but little is known of their activities after this date. We do know that the author continued to write for a number of years afterwards, but by the time of the outbreak of World War 2, he was content to serve as an air-raid warden and leave the writing of fiction in the past.

The three brothers became known locally as the 'three wise men' until William Bromley died in June 1944. The two remaining brothers stayed on in the house, and were rather secretive, but it is known that they possessed a signed photograph of the Jersey Lily, Lilly Langtry, and a letter from esteemed actress Fay Compton. It requested that should 'The Tree of the Garden' ever be dramatised, could she be considered for the role of Thursday.

Edward died from a cerebral thrombosis on July 6th 1954 at York Clifton Hospital. He was cremated in Hull and his ashes are interred in a family vault at Christ Church, Doncaster. After his brother's death and until he too died in December the same year, George Edward kept the casks of both brothers' ashes in his room. When he passed on, he left nearly £3000 to pay for a new edition of Edward's Holderness novels – 'The Cliff End' , 'The Tree of the Garden', 'Fondie' and 'The Doctor's Lass'. All profits were to go to the Imperial Cancer Fund. The books became known as the Holderness editions, and were published by Putnam's, under the guidance of John Pudney. However, it seems unlikely that the charity ever actually saw any profits from their sale.

Seaton House - the Booth brothers resided here in 1912 - 1926

Penistone Cottage in Scalby, where the Booths moved in 1926

The young Edward Booth sometimes stayed at Laurel Farm, Skeffling

SOME TRIBUTES *to the* WORK *of*
EDWARD C. BOOTH

"MR. BOOTH'S *delineations of these Holderness people is, to a reviewer who has been reading novels daily for years, the truest and most humorous picture of country life since the earlier novels of* GEORGE ELIOT."—DR. ERNEST BAKER *in* THE ATHENÆUM.

"*What* HARDY *is to Wessex, what* GEORGE ELIOT *is to the Midlands, that is* MR. BOOTH *to the East Riding of Yorkshire.*"—BIRMINGHAM POST.

"MR. BOOTH *has got the accents, the types, the manners, the gossip of Yorkshire rural life to perfection—and style to make all these things tell.*"—SUNDAY TIMES.

". . . *His use of its dialect is a triumph. Never do we remember to have reposed upon the speech of a novelist's characters with a more delightful sense of security.*"—THE OUTLOOK.

Some of the reviews in the front of 'The Treble Clef', published 1924

Winifred Holtby

This author needs little introduction to Yorkshire readers, for she is famous for her novel 'South Riding', which was published posthumously in 1936. Winifred was born at Rudston near Bridlington on June 23rd 1898. Her parents, who were prosperous farmers, were David and Alice. Her mother, involved in local politics, went on to become the first woman alderman in the East Riding of Yorkshire.

In her early years, Winifred shared a governess with the vicar's children and while still young showed literary promise, editing her own schoolroom magazine. By thirteen years of age, a selection of her poems, entitled 'My garden and other verses' was published in book form by Brown's of Hull. Winifred attended the Queen Margaret's boarding school at Scarborough and was resident there when the German warships bombarded the town on December 16th 1914.

She was happy at the school, and the head teacher, Miss Fowler, and her history mistress, Miss Crichton, were to be big influences on the budding writer. The school moved to Pitlochry in January 1915 for the duration of the war, and Winifred disliked the mountains and the separation from the rolling hills where she had grown up. Winning the Form VI prize for an essay on Kitchener in 1916, she then went on to pass the entrance exam for Somerville College, Oxford the following year.

However, Winifred instead chose to join the Women's Army Auxiliary Corps early in 1918 and went to France after first spending time training in a London nursing home. During this period, she had romantic feelings for Harry Pearson, but they never married.

When the war ended, she returned to England and took up her place at the University of Oxford in 1919. Here she met Vera Brittain, another student, who went on to become a life long friend. Fortunately for them both, from 1920 they were allowed to have degrees conferred, so in 1921, Winifred graduated with a second class degree. The author liked Oxford and started writing poetry there, and began the outline of her first novel, 'Anderby Wold'.

Her family had left Rudston in 1918, and by October 1921 they settled at 'Bainesse' in Cottingham. Winifred was also on the move, arriving at 52 Doughty Street, Bloomsbury in London the following January. By the time that she had moved further down the street, to number 58, she was performing paid work both as a teacher and a journalist. All the time, she was writing and beginning to have articles accepted. Winifred, and indeed, Vera, were both very engaged in politics, being pacifists, socialists and feminists. Indeed, Winifred was involved with the League of Nations and a number of women's causes for the rest of her life. She was active in the Independent Labour Party and was a consistent campaigner for the unionisation of black workers in South Africa. This work brought her into contact with Leonard Woolf.

By April 1922, 'Anderby Wold' was completed, and was accepted for publication by John Lane in January 1923. Winfred was a prolific letter writer, and also began work on short stories, often for the paper 'Time and Tide'. Despite her prodigious work rate, she still found time to perform many public engagements as a speaker. She even found time to attend conferences in Geneva on behalf of the League of Nations from 1923 on, for Winifred liked to travel, as did Vera. By November 1923, they both lived at 117 Wymering Mansions in Maida Vale. Winifred's second novel 'The Crowded Street', set in Yorkshire, was published in September 1924.

In 1925, Vera Brittain married George Catlin, so Winifred shared her friends' homes at Nevern Place, Earls Court and later at 19 Glebe Street, Chelsea. Winifred was her bridesmaid at the wedding, even though Catlin resented his wife's close relationship with her. Despite this apparent difficulty, Winfred went on to become adoptive aunt to Vera's two children, John and Shirley.

The author visited South Africa in both 1925 and 1926 and gave lectures, the benefits of education being a major topic, as was unionisation. By July 1926, Winifred was back in the U.K. and became director of 'Time and Tide'. Her novel 'Land of Green Ginger;' about farming post World War 1, was published in 1927. Her work rate continued to be tremendous, despite visiting Geneva every year until 1930, and helping to nurse her father in 1929, the year that a trades union was founded in South Africa.

Winifred was first ill in 1927, but her passion for fighting injustice and other causes drove her on. By 1931, she was suffering from high blood pressure, and that year she was diagnosed with Bright's disease. Her doctor gave her only two years to live, but this diagnosis did not slow her down.

In 1932, her novel 'Mandoa, Mandoa' appeared. At the same time, she was involved with four committees connected with South Africa, plus many societies involved in suffrage and education.

Her father died on March 9th 1933 at Cottingham, by which time Winifred was the book reviewer for 'Good Housekeeping', a job that she retained until her untimely demise in late 1935. She was also writing many political leaders for the 'News Chronicle' that year.

We now arrive at the time that Winifred set about writing her classic novel, 'South Riding', set in a fictional part of Yorkshire that was clearly based almost entirely on Holderness. Places of note are Hull, which becomes Kingsport, Withernsea is renamed Kiplington and Sunk Island is re-titled Cold Harbour. Slightly less flattering are the names for Hornsea – Pidsea Buttock, and Skipsea, Ledsea Buttock!

Early in 1934 the author spent three months in Withernsea, renting 34 Waxholme Road for the duration. While staying in the seaside resort, she found time to visit her mother in Cottingham and undertake research in Hull Central Library. By this time her public speaking had stopped, for she was determined to finish this title, aware that time was not on her side as the disease progressed.

The summer of 1934 found her back in London with Vera Brittain and her husband. She even managed to write more articles, attend meetings and give a few interviews, and visit Europe for a holiday. Her first collection of short stories, written between 1923 and 1933, saw the light of day as 'Truth is not sober'. It was not until after her death that her second collection was published.

Early in 1935, Winifred decamped to Hornsea, and resided at 71 Cliff Road, where she furiously continued work on 'South Riding'. She undertook lots of walks, especially to Atwick, and managed to finish the first draft of the novel before leaving the resort. Despite the advanced stage of her illness, she still found time to write more articles, particularly for 'The Schoolmistress' and the 'Journal'. Of note during this sojourn in her beloved East Riding is that she gave a talk at Hull University College on March 22nd, and addressed the Trinity Methodist School at Driffield on April 12th. Winifred even attended the N.U.T. conference at Scarborough that year.

Before summer arrived in 1935, Winifred was back in London, and incredibly at this time, still planning another trip to Africa! She corrected the final draft of her novel and went into a nursing home in September. Staying cheerful to the last, she lapsed into a coma on the 29th and died. She is buried in Rudston, Her book came out the following year with a preface dedicated to her mother. The novel garnered universal acclaim and won the James Tait Black memorial prize in 1937.

Winifred stayed at 34 Waxholme Road, Withernsea in early 1934

In 1935 the author continued her writing at 71 Cliff Road, Hornsea

John Ronald Reuel Tolkien

The most famous of the authors listed in this volume of Holderness literary worthies is J R R Tolkien, the creator of 'The Hobbit' and 'The Lord of the Rings', which are surely among the most famous works in 20th century English literature. The writer spent nearly eighteen months in Hull and Holderness during World War 1.

The author was born in South Africa, but grew up in the western suburbs of the rapidly expanding city of Birmingham with his mother, his father having died back in South Africa. He went to Oxford University and after gaining his degree, the author signed up in the town with the 13th service Battalion Lancashire Fusiliers on June 28th, 1915. He received a commission as a 2nd Lieutenant and trained for a year, including a spell in Yorkshire at the Army's Northern Command at Farnley Park, Otley in April 1916.

He went to France on June 6th 1916, serving with the 11th Battalion of the Lancashire Fusiliers. Having seen action on the Western Front, he succumbed to trench fever at Beauval on October 27th and returned to England early in November. At first he was sent to Birmingham University Wartime Hospital, then to Great Haywood and finally, after examination by the Lichfield Medical Board, to Harrogate Convalescent Hospital at the end of February 1917. Even as early as November 27th 1916, correspondence shows that the Humber garrison, based at Ottringham, were expecting him to join the 3rd Reserve Battalion Lancashire Fusiliers and assist in defending the region.

He spent most of the winter of 1916 / 1917 recovering at Great Haywood in the West Midlands. After attending several medical boards, he travelled to Harrogate, where his wife, Edith, and her cousin, Jennie Grove, had taken lodgings in March 1917.

When he had recovered sufficiently, he was initially dispatched on April 19th to the Humber Garrison at Hornsea. The 3rd Lancashire Fusiliers had an outpost and musketry school there, an encampment of wooden huts at nearby Rolston (which later became a holiday camp for boys). The camp had opened on May 23rd 1907 as a rifle range for the use of the Hull Rifle Volunteer Corps. By the 1990s the site had become derelict, and it has since become a holiday chalet park. The garrison was charged with defending the Holderness coast and the River Humber against invasion. Tolkien's wife Edith, whom he had married only the year before, followed him, and took lodgings, along with cousin Jennie, at 1 Bank Terrace, next to Hornsea Bridge railway station. There is a blue plaque attached to the property to highlight her stay. It appears that he was almost immediately posted to the battalion headquarters at Thirtle Bridge Camp, between Withernsea and Roos. Today, it is hard to envisage that a camp, capable of accommodating 1500 soldiers and 60 officers, has ever existed at this location. It had only a short existence, from 1916 until the huts were dismantled and auctioned off in August 1919. All that survives is the former cookhouse, and next to it, the former officer's mess, a much modernised bungalow, now called Mona House. After spending several weeks at Bank Terrace, Edith probably followed him to the camp at the beginning of June. There is much conjecture as to where the author and his wife stayed during those weeks in early summer 1917.

While based at Thirtle Bridge, Edith danced for Tolkien amongst the flowering hemlock at Dent's Garth at the south end of Roos village, and this event inspired a seminal story in the Middle-earth mythology – the tale of Luthien Tinýviel and Beren. This episode in 1917 made such an impression upon the young author, that towards the end of his life, and after Edith had died, he commented that Roos was the most significant place in this world that helped inspire the legendary world that he was to create. Indeed, Holderness was to have a considerable influence on him, with its isolation and the continual erosion of the vulnerable coast helping to inspire the legendarium that he ultimately expounded.

On July 12th, while her husband was still based at Thirtle Bridge, Edith moved to digs at 76 Queen Street, Withernsea, in what is now the southern part of the Lifeboat Cafe. Again, there is now a blue plaque above the door to commemorate her stay in the seaside resort. For a short while in July, the author went down to Dunstable via Hornsea, to undertake a signalling exam. On his journey down south or on his return, he temporarily had digs at what is now 79 Cliff Road, but was then named 'Waverley'.

Despite his astonishing aptitude for languages, he failed this test and returned to Thirtle Bridge. Tolkien attended a regimental dinner on August 1st with his friend Huxtable, a fellow officer, who was staying at nearby Tunstall Hall, but became ill and fell into a fever. He was immediately transferred to Brooklands Officers' Hospital on Cottingham Road, Hull, which had only opened a matter of days before. The building still exists today as the Dennison Centre, the University of Hull's International Office, and is now adorned by a plaque to commemorate the author's stay there. Meanwhile, Edith, who was now pregnant, resided in Withernsea until August 21st, when she departed from Yorkshire and headed south to Cheltenham. During his stay in Hull, Tolkien started to write 'The Tale of Tinýviel', the story inspired by his wife's dancing at Roos earlier that year, 'The Fall of Gondolin' and also began drafting 'The Tale of Turambar'. It is at this time that Tolkien, using the languages that he was then inventing, alludes to Withernsea as 'Tol Withernon'. 'Tol' in one of the author's created languages means 'island'. Having undertaken look-out duties at Sand-le-Mere, with the Tunstall drain only yards away, he must have perceived how easy it would be to cut off south Holderness if the German Ocean, as it was known then, broke though at that point.

While he was convalescing in Hull hospital, the writer was befriended by Sister Mary Michael, a member of the local Sisters of Mercy. Their base was Endsleigh House on Beverley Road, and she was to remain a lifelong friend of Tolkien, even becoming godmother to the author's second son, Michael, who was born in 1920.

Even while recuperating at the hospital in Hull, another Holderness connection can be noted. The hospital was under the jurisdiction of

Mrs Margaret Strickland Constable, of Wassand Hall, Hornsea. She also had charge of the Red Cross military hospital at Hornsea. Interestingly for Tolkien, she was fluent in several languages, just at the time that the author was himself attempting to improve his knowledge of Spanish, Italian and even Russian!

Discharged from Brooklands in October, he returned to light duties at Thirtle Bridge Camp. Tolkien had to attend a number of medical boards during his stay in East Yorkshire, and for this purpose, it would appear that he travelled to see the Humber Garrison medical officers, who were based at 130 Anlaby Road, near Hull Paragon station. On the date of one such board, November 16th, his wife gave birth to their first child, John, in Cheltenham, and there is considerable conjecture whether after recovering the mother and child joined him in Holderness later that month. However, Tolkien was still receiving medical care, and was promptly transferred to the headquarters of the 9th Battalion, Royal Defence Corps, an organisation similar to the Home Guard in the Second World War, at Easington. The appropriate medical treatment was administered at the hospital on Fort Godwin, an army camp at nearby Kilnsea, which is now the Sandy Beaches caravan park. While staying at what Tolkien described as 'a lonely house near Easington', he continued work on stories that ultimately would become part of 'The Book of Lost Tales'. In December, while he was billeted here, Tolkien was promoted to Lieutenant.

After attending yet another medical board on March 19th 1918, Tolkien ended his treatment, and also his service with the Royal Defence Corps (which was by then being run down), and returned to the 3rd Lancashire Fusiliers at his former base at Thirtle Bridge. He was not to stay there long though, for on April 10th he was considered fighting fit, and was posted to Cannock Chase, Staffordshire. However, he had not finished with East Yorkshire yet, for at the end of June he contracted gastritis at Brocton camp, and was sent back for treatment once more to Brooklands Hospital in Hull. On July 26th Tolkien received orders to go to Boulogne immediately, but fortunately the order was cancelled, and this left him with several months in Hull to develop his writing further. By this date his wife was residing in Cheltenham. The great writer was to stay at the Brooklands Officers' Hospital until September 11th, when he was transferred to the Savoy Convalescent Hospital in Blackpool until the end of the war.

So ended the war service of the creator of 'The Hobbit' and 'Lord of the Rings', much of which had been spent in Holderness and the East Riding of Yorkshire. Had his health been slightly better, the author might have been sent back to France, and met the fate shared by so many of his countrymen on those foreign fields. His stay in the area not only influenced his mythology, but also probably saved his life. Without sojourns in Hull and Holderness, the 20th century might have been deprived of one of its most famous and influential literary figures.

J R R Tolkien in his lieutenant's uniform in 1916

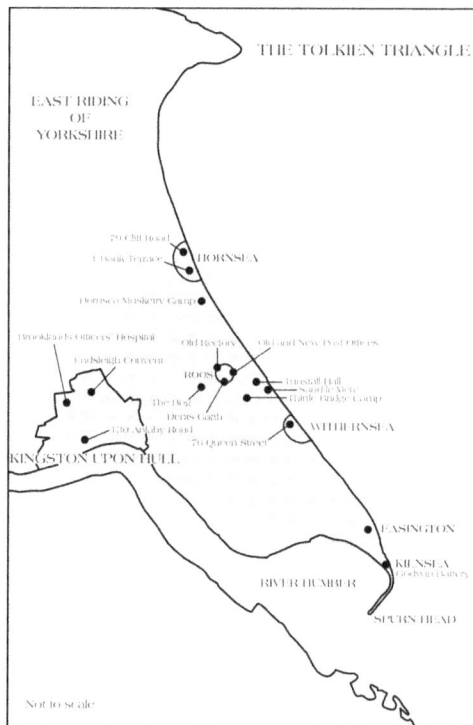

The Tolkien Triangle - the Hull & Holderness connections

Oliver Onions

The author was born as George Oliver Onions on November 13th 1873 in Bradford, West Yorkshire. His parents were George Frederick Onions, who worked as a cashier in a bank, and Emily Alice Fearnley. George Frederick had been born in London in 1847 and in 1850 Emily entered the world at a place called Scholes in Yorkshire. After school George Oliver studied art at the National Arts Training School in London, and worked as a draughtsman. He was a fellow with a number of interests, such as motoring, science and even boxing as an amateur. In his time as a designer, he created books and posters. While working as a commercial artist, he assisted in illustrating the Boer War in magazines. It would appear that his future lay with illustrating, but an American author, Gelett Burgess, encouraged Onions to start writing fiction. The first editions of his earliest novels have full colour dust wrappers painted by the author himself.

He soon started to make his mark, for then only in his late twenties, he had several novels published, such as 'the Compleat Bachelor' in 1900; 'Tales from a Far Riding' in 1902 and 'The Odd-Job Man' following in 1903. In total he wrote at least thirty novels. By the time of his next novel in 1906 'The Drakestone', his first collection of short stories had appeared. Entitled 'Back o' the Moon', it contained five stories, including the eponymous one of the title. Omnibus volumes soon appeared, 'Admiral Eddy' being the first one in 1907, to be followed by four more during his long and distinguished writing career.

In 1909, Onions married the Welsh author (but born in India), Berta Ruck, and they became Mr and Mrs Onions. However, George changed his name to George Oliver in 1918, and so the couple spent the rest of their lives as Mr & Mrs Oliver. For the benefit of their readers, George still retained his established author's name of Oliver Onions, and Berta continued as Berta Ruck. It would appear that

Onions helped Ruck to revise her story 'His Official Fiancée', which had appeared in 1912 as a serial in 'Home Chat' for distribution in book form. The novel was published in 1914, and was a success on both sides of the Atlantic. Thus, Berta's long and prolific career as a writer was secured, for she went on to publish over ninety romantic novels, and outlived her husband by a number of years, not passing away until 1978 when she was one hundred years old. They had two sons, Arthur was born in 1912, with William born the following year. The author appears to have been a rather private individual, not moving in the traditional literary circles. Therefore, there are few personal memoirs of him that have survived.

He is best known for ghost stories, particularly the collection 'Widdershins', published in 1911. This book included the tale 'The Beckoning Fair One', which became widely anthologized. However, he also wrote in other styles such as science fiction, fantasy, horror and detective stories. The story that we are interested in, 'The Story of Ragged Robyn', probably falls into the category of historical crime. The title was published by Michael Joseph & Son in 1945, and is the story of Robyn Skyme and set in the late seventeenth century. It involves a gang led by the legendary bandit queen, Peg Fyfe of Yorkshire folklore, and concerns a promise made by the young Robyn to this vicious 'Queen of Holderness'. He lives in North Lincolnshire, before becoming apprenticed to a certain Hendryk Maas to become a stonemason. His travels then take him all over Yorkshire, but of interest to us is the significant mention of Mocklington, which is clearly Patrington, where the master and apprentice undertake work. Also of note within the tale is the mention of Sunk Island, the 'Earls of Hornsea', the 'Prince of Withernsea' and the 'Duke of Spurn'. The story ends gruesomely at 'Intake', which is clearly on the Holderness coast. There is an Intake just south of Withernsea, so that is another significant local reference. The book is a romp across Lincolnshire with several references to crossing the Humber, travelling to York and the Wolds, and journeying from Goole to Holderness via North Cave.

Onions' work was largely well received, impressing such distinguished authors as Algernon Blackwood, A M Burrage, J B Priestley and the acclaimed supernatural author Robert Aickman. All considered that he assisted in bringing the phantoms of the past from scary castles and gothic scenarios to the normal living rooms of the readers. However, not all agreed, for the famous writer L P Lovecraft did not rate his work very highly. Nevertheless, his lifetime of successful creativity was eventually recognized when he was awarded the James Tait Black Memorial Prize for one of his last tales, the 1946 novel 'Poor Man's Tapestry'.

Having spent much of his life in Wales, the author died on the 9th April 1961 in Aberystwyth. His final novel 'A Shilling to Spend' was published posthumously in 1965.

Oliver Onions in the early 20th century

Plaque on Hubert Nicholson's birthplace, 37 Washington St, Hull

Hubert Nicholson

Our next author, Hubert Nicholson, was born in Hull on January 23rd 1908, and lived at 37 Washington Street, Beverley Road. From an early age he visited Holderness and considered it his 'dearest location', often staying in cottages at Ryehill, Thorngumbald and Ottringham.

He was the son of a master printer and left school at sixteen years of age. His father would have liked him to follow in his line of work, but Hubert was keen to work in newspapers. He started as a copy-runner between the sub-editors' room and the composing room. Initially, he was employed at the 'Eastern Morning News' group, which also published the 'Hull News' on a Saturday. He soon graduated to journalism, which had always been his ambition. When the actress and author Colette O'Neil, real name Lady Constance Malleson, joined the Hull Repertory Theatre Company for a season in 1925, Hubert introduced her to Holderness, which with her Irish background, she loved.

Despite the promising start to his career, the newspaper company that he worked for went out of business in 1930. For a while he was unemployed, but then joined the team at the 'Hull Daily Mail'. His role as film critic gave him the opportunity to view hundreds of movies, but he was also a general reporter for the paper. It was at this time that he developed a desire to travel, so he started to venture further than Scarborough and Whitby for his holidays. He had frequent trips to London to enjoy the Bohemian atmosphere, especially around Soho, and also went to the Continent.

Leaving Hull in 1933, he resided in Bristol, where he began working for 'The Evening World' newspaper. He then settled in Cheltenham to work on the 'Gloucestershire Echo' but disliked the job. In December 1934, he returned to Hull to marry his local sweetheart, Molly, at the registry Office. The following year his first collection of poems, 'Date' was printed. It subsequently sold out, and he already had a novel accepted for publication.

Molly and Hubert then moved to London in the summer of 1936, settling in Bloomsbury. This was much more to his taste, and he became immersed in the life of Fleet Street. Initially, he was employed by the 'Sunday Dispatch'. His work as a journalist brought him into contact with many famous people, such as George Bernard Shaw, Sir Thomas Beecham, the Sitwells, W.H. Auden, Dylan Thomas, and even Louis Armstrong! However, his marriage was already in trouble, and the couple divorced soon after a stay in Hull at Christmas 1937. Hubert returned to London and settled in Hampstead. Eventually, he married the novelist Barbara Collard, and she bore him two sons and a daughter. Tragically, the elder son committed suicide and as a result of this, the author wrote his longest poem, 'Monody - to my son Paul: 1939 – 1982'.

His biography 'Half my Days and Nights', published in 1941, provides us with his story up to this point. In World War 2 he worked in a factory metal-casting, and then returned to Fleet Street again. The writer joined Reuters, the news agency, in 1945 and worked there until his retirement in 1968. By this date he was the senior sub-editor. During his career he met an immense number of characters in the creative and literary fields. In retirement he intended to write the second part of his autobiography, but he never did.

During the 1950s, Nicholson turned his considerable literary creativity to two novels that indicate his long time affection for Holderness. In 1954, the title 'Little Heyday' was published by Heinemann. Set in the fictional village of Sweynby, which geographically appears to be near Burstwick, it is a tale of life in a farming community on the cusp of the First World War. Local dialect is in evidence in the work. There are many mentions of the lost towns of the Yorkshire coast and within the Humber estuary. Indeed, there are numerous references to well known Holderness historical facts. Many villages are named – Thorngumbald, Hedon, Sunk Island, Skeffling, Burton Pidsea are just a sample of locations listed in the narrative.

In 1956, the author revisited Holderness in his literature once more. This time, the tale 'Sunk Island', again published by Heinemann, was a contemporary one. The 1953 storm surge and subsequent flooding had created considerable difficulties for the inhabitants of this low lying piece of land. Again, a number of local locations are mentioned, such as Paull, Keyingham, Ryehill and Kelsey Hill, but with fictional people populating the pages. The action takes place once again within a farming family, and is a rather dark saga.

Later in life, he decided to become the literary executor of the poet, A S J Tessimond, and edited two posthumous collections of this poet's work - 'Not love perhaps' in 1978, and 'Morning Meeting' in 1980. By this time he had developed diabetes, and the condition was to severely restrict his life from then on. In later years he often welcomed friends from an armchair, but remained active until his demise by using a wheelchair. His final address was in Epsom, and from his cottage he was admitted to hospital in November 1995. His death occurred on January 11th 1996.

In his lifetime he had over thirty books published, including poetry, twelve novels, books of criticism and plays.

Robin Skelton

This writer and poet was born in Easington on October 12th 1925, in the schoolhouse where his father, Cyril Frederick William was the teacher. His mother was Lili, and he was to be an only child. He was educated at this school until he was nearly eleven, when he went on to Pocklington Grammar School as a boarding pupil.

When he left school in 1943 he was sponsored by the RAF for a six month course for potential officers at Christ's College, Cambridge. He spent most of his war service as a sergeant in India, working as a codes and cipher clerk. After demobilization in 1947, he went to Leeds University to study English Literature, gaining a First Class Honours B.A. in 1950, and an M.A. the following year.

Between 1951 and 1963, the writer worked at the University of Manchester, first as an assistant lecturer and then as a full lecturer. Robin married his first wife, Margaret Lambert in 1953, but they soon divorced. In 1957, he married his second wife, Sylvia Mary Snow, and they had three children, Nicholas, Alison and Brigid. It was during his time at Manchester that his literary and artistic activities grew. Having been involved as a student with a small publishing house called Lotus Press, he continued to manage this until 1952.

His first collection of poetry, called 'Patmos and other Poems' was published in 1955. Further collections were soon to follow – 'Third Day Lucky' appeared in 1958, then 'Begging the Dialect' appeared in 1960, and by 1962, 'The Dark Window'. He supplemented his income by undertaking part time work as poetry reviewer and theatre critic for the 'Manchester Guardian'. Additionally, he was an examiner for the Northern Universities Matriculation Board and then became Chairman of Examiners for its English 'O' level examination.

Being a gregarious person, Robin met many of the leading poets of his age, including William Empson, Louis MacNeice, David Gascoyne, and Kathleen Raine. Publishing a book on versification called 'The Poetic Pattern' in 1956, he became well known to artists and writers in the Manchester area, and was involved in the founding of the Peterloo Group, along with Michael Seward Snow and Tony Connor. After this, he helped to found the Manchester Institute of Contemporary Arts, drafting its constitution and becoming its first secretary. He journeyed to Dublin in 1960 to research the playwright, J M Synge, and quickly developed a lifelong affection and empathy for Ireland and its writers. This interest in Irish literature led to the publication in 1962 of an anthology called 'Six Irish Poets'.

A turning point came in 1963, when Robin and his family emigrated to Canada for him to take up a job as Associate Professor in the University of Victoria, British Columbia. As a recently opened establishment, it was a stimulating environment for him, and he soon became engaged in a multitude of activities – poetry, editing, literary and dramatic criticism, art, anthology, administration and teaching. He was promoted to full Professor of English in 1966, and between 1967 and 1973 was the director of the newly created 'Creative Writing Program' which he had inaugurated. In the latter year, the facility became the Department of Creative Writing and Robin was its chairman until 1976.

The 1970s were very productive years for the writer. Having founded the 'Malahat Review' in 1967, initially he was its joint editor and then sole editor from 1972 to 1983. Fortunately, his work in the country did not go unrecognized, for in 1981 he took up the role as Vice-Chairman and then became full Chairman of the Writers' Union of Canada in 1982 - 1983. Robin's interest in publishing also continued, acting as editor-in-chief to a couple of small presses in Victoria, the 'Sono Nis Press' from 1967 to 1982, and subsequently 'Pharos Press' from 1972 onwards. He also exhibited several one-man collage shows in the city during 1966, 1968 and 1980.

He was a prodigious writer, with over one hundred titles to his credit.

Apart from his work on the Irish literary scene, he also wrote books on the craft of poetry, such as 'The Practice of Poetry' in 1971, 'The Poet's Calling' in 1975 and 'The Shapes of our Singing' published posthumously in 2002. Robin also edited a number of anthologies, such as 'Poetry of the Thirties' in 1964, and 'Poetry of the Forties' in 1968 for the Penguin Press.

However, it is for his own poetry that he is best remembered. His earliest poem that speaks of his Holderness roots appears to be 'Humber-side, 1939,' which mentions Spurn. It would seem that Robin was first published in a student magazine at Christ's College, Cambridge. Initially, his work in the 1950s and early 1960s was classed as being of the New Movement style, but he then established his own style. This development was to appear in longer verse such as 'Timelight' in 1974 and 'Callsigns' two years later. His later work then became shorter and brighter, 'Popping Fuchsias' of 1992 and 'One Leaf Shaking' from 1996 demonstrating this. His childhood in Holderness often informed his writing, with some poems referencing places from his formative years. Examples of this are the poems 'Dimlington Heights', 'Dirty Snow', with its mention of the Hildyard Arms at Patrington, and no less than three references to his old schoolhouse in Easington in the works 'The Red House', 'Change but no change' and 'All of Us There Once'. Skelton experimented with many diverse poetic forms, such as those of Japan and Wales, but he also created a few of his own.

The writer, always impressive, was also noted as rather an eccentric figure, and could strike fear into students initially. Once they got past this initial impression, they soon realized that he was kind and humble. His persona could be likened to that of an ancient Druid, and indeed, he was interested in the occult and Wicca. In later years he had a long beard and white hair, rings, tattoos and a talismanic pentagram. He scorned convention and conformity and proceeded to publish a number of books on witchcraft, such as 'Spellcraft' in 1978, 'Talismanic Magic' in 1985 and finally in 1988, 'The Practice of Witchcraft Today'.

His autobiography, entitled 'The Memoirs of a Literary Blockhead' was published in 1988, and in it he bemoaned the lack of recognition in his native England, for by this time he had received honours in the country which he had adopted as his own back in 1963. He died at home in Victoria after a short illness brought on by complications resulting from diabetes and congestive heart failure, on August 27th 1997. He was seventy one years old.

Many thanks to Jan Crowther for kind permission to use her husband Peter's article as the basis for this chapter.

Robin Skelton was born in the Old Schoolhouse, Easington in 1925

Robin Skelton in the mid 1980s

In celebration of other literary worthies

Having focused on a number of literary figures, mention should now be made of a plethora of other writers worthy of note with regard to Holderness.

The earliest mention of Holderness in literature is in Geoffrey Chaucer's 'Canterbury Tales', written in the 14th century. One of these stories - 'The Summoner's Tale' contains the following rhyming couplets starting at line 45 of the text:

'Masters, there is in Yorkshire, as I guess,
A marshy region that's called Holderness,
Wherein there went a limiter about
To preach, and to beg too, beyond a doubt....'

Our most famous playwright, Shakespeare, mentions the lost seaport of Ravenspurn no less than eight times in three of his plays. Here are the references: Richard II, Act 2, Scene 1; Richard II, Act 2, Scene 2; Richard II, Act 2, Scene 3 twice; Henry IV Part 1, Act 1, Scene 3; Henry IV Part 1, Act 3, Scene 2; Henry IV Part 1, Act 4, Scene 3; Henry VI Part 3, Act 4, Scene 7.

From the same period we can add the poet, Michael Drayton, who was born near Nuneaton in 1563 and died in 1631. In 1598, he started a topographical poem that became entitled 'Poly-Olbion'. Published in 1612, it was reprinted in 1622 with a second part. Running to almost fifteen thousand lines of verse, it contained lines about all parts of England. Of note to us are the following passages from book 28, describing Kilnsea and Spurn:

'Then note upon the south,
How all along the shore, to mighty Humber's mouth,

Rich Holderness I have, excelling for her grain.'
So I my course, maintain
From Kilnsey's pyle-like point, along the eastern shore,
And laugh at Neptune's rage, when loudest he doth roar,
Till Flamborough jut forth into the German sea'

Ravenser, or Ravenspurn, has captured the imagination of several writers, especially in poetry. In the 1885 Hull Christmas Annual, J Campbell Thompson published a poem called 'Ravenser'. In 1953, it was the turn of Donald Gordon Hart to publish 'The Lost Town of Ravenserodd' in 'Humberside', the journal of the Hull Literary Club. As we shall see later, a number of this club's members were writers of Holderness related material. Finally, I have discovered a further poem by Claire Ellin of Kilnwick, who sent her poem 'Ravenspurn' to Hull University lecturer George De Boer in 1961.

However, when the literature of Holderness and particularly Ravenser is mentioned, one book consistently appears, 'The Lord of the Ravens' by Paul Bourquin. This is a novel set in the lost seaport of Ravenser Odd, and has the sub-title, 'A Tale of a vanished town'. We can do no better than quote the descriptive text inside the dustwrapper cover to get the substance of the narrative – "Martin of Ulrome was no ordinary priest; and when he came to Ravenserodd, a small town at the end of a narrow causeway dividing the River Humber from the North Sea, on that spring afternoon in 1339, he came to no ordinary parish. His predecessor had been murdered, and Martin was determined to find out why, and by whom." The crafty mayor is John de la Pole, and the author expounds that 'the natural employment for Ravenserodd and its people was …. piracy.' So we see that it is a thriller mystery played out in the dying days of this famous lost Yorkshire port. However, the writer behind this book, and at least five other historical novels, is an even greater mystery. Paul Bourquin, whose real name was Richard Amberley, was born in London in 1916. After his childhood, which was mostly spent in Egypt, he was educated in England and Belgium. In 1954 he moved to 9 Broughton Road, Otford, just north of Sevenoaks in Kent. He had a wife and three daughters. Like 'The Lord of the Ravens', which was his first book in 1961, the next five titles were all published by Faber & Faber. The other stories are 'Beltane Fires' 1964; 'The Cockpit' 1965; 'The Seven Reductions' 1967; 'The Land of Delight' 1967 and 'Phocas the Gardener' in 1969.

There is one further novel, 'Dead on the Stone', but this is accredited to Richard Amberley and not the nom de plume and was published by Richard Hale in 1969. Whether this writer is one and the same as Paul Bourquin, we do not know. For an author published by a large London publishing house, his private life continues to remain a complete mystery. As a London man who spent his formative years abroad, how did he come to choose a Holderness town lost six hundred years before as the source material to launch his literary career? We shall never know, for he died in 2009.

One writer who did not get the opportunity to realise his full potential was Hull author Dan Billany. Born on November 14th 1913 at 51 Essex Street, Hessle Road, his life was cut short in World War 2. He fought in Italy, and disappeared there in 1944. A favourite haunt in his formative years was Leven in Holderness. He spent many happy days there on a house boat on the canal. The location inspired an unpublished novel of his written in 1936 called, 'A season of calm weather'. The story involves homosexuality, so it understandable that it would not find a ready publisher at that time. The location is Sedgeley, which is a thinly disguised Leven. He went on to achieve some recognition with his books 'The Opera House Murder (Faber & Faber 1940); The Magic Door (Thomas Nelson & Son 1943); 'The Cage' (Longmans Green & Co 1949) and 'The Trap' (Faber & Faber 1950).

The name Reckitt is familiar to all Hull citizens. One member of this well known family wrote a book entitled 'Brothers at Arms', set in the Civil War in 1642, and published by Highgate Publications in 1991. Its author was Basil Norman Reckitt, born in St. Albans on August 12th 1905, to Norman and Beatrice. He was educated at

Uppingham and then King's College, Cambridge. Entering the family business, he rose to be chairman of Reckitt & Colman Limited by 1966. Holderness is mentioned in the first line of the book, as is a fictional 'Rous Hall', but apart from a reference to Hedon on page 38, the location seems almost incidental to the narrative. There was also a follow up novel called 'Petronella'. Basil died on the 3rd of December 2005.

The Hull Literary Club included members with literary inclinations, who often chose Holderness as the backdrop for their poems and stories. One such writer was Ernest A Parsons, who resided at 10 Whitehall Gardens, Victoria Avenue, Hull. By 1922 he was the honorary secretary of the society, and wrote at least two Holderness tales for the Hull Daily Mail. One such tale was entitled 'The Belle of Easington' and was reproduced in 'The Hull Times' between October 10th and November 27th 1920. Prior to this date, the Hull Literary Club, in their yearbook, published 'Transition: a Story of Holderness dialect', from a talk that he had given to the club on December 6th 1915. I also discovered further work in the October 1932 edition of 'Humberside'. This was the annual journal of the Hull Literary Club. Under the chapter called 'Holderness Sketches' are three short stories – 'A Winter's Tale; ' 'Enry Downship's Legal Rights' and 'The Wizard'. Similarly, Maurice Philips, who was on the sub-committee, published a poem 'In Holderness' in the October 1923 edition of 'Humberside'.

Another leading light in the Hull Literary Club was John Redwood Anderson. He became club president in 1925 / 1926 and ultimately he was listed as an honorary member for life. His poem 'April in Holderness' is to be found in a small volume called 'In Praise of Yorkshire' published by Frederick Muller Ltd of London in 1951, but he wrote a number of other poems about Holderness. In 1935, there was 'The Old Windmills of Holderness, and in 1937 'The Towers' about Hedon and Patrington churches. Additionally, his 1955 poem 'Spurn Light' is of note. Eventually, he had twenty three books of his poetry and criticism published, starting in 1904 with 'The Music of Death', and in 1927 he even had a play, 'Babel', published.

Born in Salford in 1883, Anderson studied Theology and Philosophy at Lampeter College Oxford. He travelled widely, even before the Great War and was an accomplished violinist, having been schooled at the Brussels Conservatoire. Neither by training or inclination was he a schoolmaster, but nevertheless he was employed as such for many years at Hymers College until he left the city to reside in Corwen, Wales in 1943. Most of his considerable body of poetry was written while he sojourned in Hull. He could claim to have many nationally known writers as his friends, such as J C Powys, Lascelles Abercrombie and W W Gibson. At the time of his demise on March 29th 1964, he was resident in Sible Hedingham, Essex.

No work about poetry in the East Riding of Yorkshire could fail to mention Philip Larkin, the University of Hull librarian who went on to national fame. He often cycled around Holderness, and two plaques, one at Patrington church and one at Spurn Point acknowledge his love for this corner of England. His poem 'Here', completed in 1961, is the opening poem in 'Whitsun Weddings', published in 1964. It is about a journey from Hull to Spurn, though neither place is mentioned. Holderness and Spurn are also referenced in the work 'A Rumoured City'.

Another poet closely associated with the region is Ted Hughes, who spent part of his national service stationed with the R.A.F. at Patrington in 1950. His poem 'Mayday in Holderness' first appeared in his collection 'Lupercal' in 1960. He was born Edward James Hughes on August 17th 1930 at 1 Aspinall Street, Mytholmroyd in West Yorkshire. Aged seven years, he moved to Mexborough, where his father ran a newsagent's shop. The period that we are primarily interested in is his national service between 1949 and 1951, after which he completed his education at Pembroke College University.

At Patrington, he was part of a three man radio station as a ground wireless mechanic. This ground control radio station was known colloquially as "the Happidrome". Its purpose was to guide night fighters to attack Russian bombers. When the poet first arrived at the base, there was no accommodation for RAF staff, so he lodged with the Snaith family at number two, Northside. He would have slept on an RAF bed in the downstairs front room of the terraced house.

The earliest poem he kept from that time was titled "Song". The poem was written soon after his period of national service began, probably early 1950, when the poet was just nineteen years old. The story is that Ted became friendly with a young lady, Enid Wilkinson, who lived opposite his billet, and that he spent his off duty evenings with her. Here they would sit and talk by the fireside of her family home. During one such evening, Ted noticed and picked up an exercise book belonging to her. In it she had written down some of her favourite romantic poems. On noting this, the future Poet Laureate asked, "Shall I write you one of my poems?" Into this simple notebook he wrote the words to "Song" and another poem which, until recently, remained unpublished. The poem "Song" was included in his first collection, published in 1957 and entitled "Hawk in the Rain". Interestingly, Enid's copy contains an additional verse. The writer finished his national service days in October 1951, by which time he was probably based at RAF Fylingdales.

Finally, on the subject of poetry, I will mention David Collinson, born on Humber Lane, Welwick in 1912. He was the third of eight children, and was only four years old when his father died. His mother passed away just eight years later and he was sent to the Hesslewood orphanage. He ran away and was apprehended, but the second time he escaped he found employment as a farm lad at Dalton Holme Farm. He combined humour with his knowledge of local dialect, and was published in several literary magazines and nationals. Indeed, his poem 'The Old Wooden Plough' was featured in the 'Daily Herald' in 1955. He died in Halsham residential home at the age of eighty four years in 1997.

Several other authors are associated with East Yorkshire and the Yorkshire Coast. One such is J E Buckrose, whose real name was Annie Edith Foster. She was born in Hull in 1868, educated at Dresden and passed away in 1931. She wrote many works of fiction, but the one most frequently mentioned locally is 'Down our Street', published by Herbert Jenkins. However, it is not set in Holderness, for the action takes place in 'Flodmouth' which can be identified as Scarborough. 'Cliffborough' and even Harrogate are described in the novel, but they are obviously outside the subject of this book.

The title 'Mary Anerley' by R D Blackmore and published as a three volume novel in 1880 is of local interest, but it is set in the North Riding and with action at Flamborough Head, once again the book falls outside the scope of this work.

Similarly, Thomas Armstrong, a well known Yorkshire novelist who wrote 'The face of a Madonna', is considered of local interest. There is some validity in the inclusion of this title, published by Collins in 1964, as although the bulk of the narrative takes place in North Yorkshire, there is mention of the death of Simon of Hedon. Additionally, Sir John de Roos and his lady get a mention, and there is a portion of the book on the monks of Rievaulx travelling to the Gilbertine Priory of Watton.

The famous writer Robert Louis Stevenson was brought to my attention as having one possible title for inclusion, since the story 'The Black Arrow' appears to have several Holderness references. However, even though the story, set in the War of the Roses in the late 15th century, makes mention of Tunstall Moat House, there are no significant clues in the body of the text that this is indeed our own Tunstall. The hinterland described is indeed marshland, as Holderness was back then, but the details are too vague to state with confidence that the novel is actually set in East Yorkshire. The book was originally published in 1888.

As mentioned in my book 'Sails, Paddles and Rails – How the outside world came to Spurn Point in times gone by', I discovered one work of fiction that alludes to intrepid travellers to the peninsula from across the Humber in the 19th century. An author with the enigmatic name, E.L.F., wrote a book entitled 'Our Home in the Marsh Land' which was published by Griffith Farran Browne & Co of London in 1877. The narrative follows some young folk who cross the Humber from the marshlands of North Lincolnshire to enjoy the delights of Spurn and its lighthouses, having never been there before.

Another writer I discovered was H Brierley, who published a story in the Hull Times on July 6th 1895 entitled 'The mad maid of Kilnsea'. This author was probably Harwood Brierley, who tended to write articles on topographical matters, such as one about Patrington and Hedon churches.

T E Lawrence, better known as Lawrence of Arabia, must rank as one of the most famous entries in this book. However, he wrote predominantly non-fiction, such as accounts of his time in World War 1, the Arab world and also his time in the R.A.F. Despite this being outside the scope of this book, he did also produce some poetry, so let us look a little more closely at this fascinating man's connection with Holderness. I am indebted to S F Taylor's volume called 'This Squalid Little Room - Lawrence of Arabia' for details of his time spent in Hornsea.

Thomas Edward Lawrence was born on the 16th August 1888 in Tremadoc in North Wales. His parents, Thomas Lawrence and Sarah Junner never married, and the stigma of being illegitimate remained with him all his life. The family moved to Kircudbright, Scotland, the Isle of Man and St Helier in the Channel Islands, before settling in Oxford. Here, the young T E Lawrence went to school and then attended Jesus College, Oxford, gaining a 1st class degree in history in 1910. His career in World War 1 is well known, especially his exploits against the Turks in the Middle East. After the conflict, his fame quickly proved a burden to him, and he changed his name to T E Shaw in 1923. Soon after this time he joined the Royal Air Force as a first class aircraftman.

He was assigned to a detachment at Bridlington, which had a base at Catfoss, just six miles west of Hornsea. Here, T E Shaw met Flight Lieutenant Reginald G Sims. The two became friends after the author was posted to East Yorkshire on November 15th 1934. Lawrence frequently visited Reginald and his wife, Hilda and son, John at their home, White Cottage, No3 Eastgate, Hornsea. He even stayed over and obviously felt at ease with the family. He attended orchestral concerts in Hull and visited local sites such as Beverley Minster. However, his time with the R.A.F. was coming to an end, and on February 26th 1935 he left the forces and the area, returning to his home, Clouds Hill in Dorset. While riding his motorcycle locally on the 19th of May that year, he was in an accident and died. He was just forty six years of age.

Before we leave this chapter, mention must be made of one Yorkshire literary family who ultimately achieved world wide fame – the Brontes. Charlotte Bronte spent a considerable period on the Yorkshire Coast, which she loved. She was the third daughter of six children born to Rev. Patrick Bronte, and entered this world on April 21st 1816 in Thornton, West Yorkshire.

After leaving the Cowan Bridge school for clergymen's daughters, together with the other two surviving Brontes, Emily and Anne, she started writing childish stories and articles for magazines. Charlotte later attended Miss Wooler's school at Roe Head, and became friends with Ellen Nussey of Birstall, who became a lifelong friend.

Charlotte then became a teacher herself, before being employed as a governess to Mr John Sidgwick, a wealthy industrialist living near Skipton. Unhappy at this line of employment, she returned home, and at this time, Ellen suggested a holiday, initially at Cleethorpes.

However, Ellen's brother had just left Burton Agnes, where he had been acting as a curate to Rev Charles Henry Lutwidge (he was the uncle of Charles Lutwidge Dodgson, better known as Lewis Carroll). Therefore their plans changed and they headed off to stay with the Hudson family at Easton, near Bridlington in September 1839.

Charlotte was much excited by the prospect of a coastal holiday, and this was the first of several to the Yorkshire coast. The two ladies returned home in October, and once again, Charlotte became a governess, this time to a Bradford merchant, Mr John White, who lived at Rawdon. She even considered setting up a school near Bridlington, but first Emily died in December 1848, and then Anne followed on May 28th 1849 while at Scarborough.

Therefore, Charlotte revisited the Hudsons at Easton in June 1849, and did much writing there. In June 1852, she added Filey to her tally of Yorkshire resorts. Finally, in September 1853, Charlotte arrived at Hornsea, staying with an old friend, Margaret Wooler. She was very happy in this seaside town, an attitude expressed in her letters at the time. Unfortunately, the author never managed another visit to the Holderness coast, for she died not long after her marriage to Rev. Arthur Bell Nicholls, on March 31st 1855.

The 14th century writer, Geoffrey Chaucer

The Hull author John Redwood Anderson

Paul Bourquin, the writer of 'The Lord of the Ravens'

Patrington Haven camp, where Ted Hughes was stationed in 1950

Bibliography

Armstrong, Thomas – The Face of a Madonna, Collins 1964

Around the Wolds and North Yorkshire, Issue 67, July – August 1999

Birrell, Augustine – English men of letters : Andrew Marvell, Macmillan & Co 1905

Bourquin, Paul – Lord of the Ravens : A tale of a vanished town, Faber & Faber 1961

Braddon, Mary Elizabeth – Lady Audley's secret, with new introduction by Norman Donaldson, Dover Publications 1979

Beckwith, Frank – Yorkshire Historical Fiction, Dalesman Publishing Company 1947

Buckrose, J E – Down our Street, Herbert Jenkins 1911

Crowther, Peter – Robin Skelton, article unpublished

English, Barbara – Extraordinary women of Beverley, Beverley Civic Society 2019

Flit – How to be happy though hunted, from the foxes' point of view, A Brown & Sons

Flit & Ko – A Holderness Harvest, A Brown & Sons

Foster, Catherine & Florence – The Goblin, Wells, Gardners, Darton & Co 1900

Dewhurst, John – The laureate of Holderness, Edward Charles Booth : A literary quest 2008 L920 BOO

Leckonby, P A & Hall, H M – Holmpton : A Journey Through Time, Artisan Desktop Publishing no date

Hubert, Nicholson – Half my days and nights, Autolycus Publications 1982

Hubert, Nicholson – Little Heyday, Heinemann 1954

Hubert, Nicholson – Sunk Island, Heinemann 1956

Macdonald, Mary – Notes on the life and work of E C Booth (from research by John Munday) 1995

Mathison, Phil – Tolkien in East Yorkshire 1917 – 1918, Dead Good Publications 2012

Onions, Oliver – The Story of Ragged Robyn, Chatto & Windas 1945 Michael Joseph Ltd 1945

Pearson, F R – Charlotte Brontë on the East Yorkshire Coast, The East Yorkshire Local History Society 1987

Reid, Christopher – Letters of Ted Hughes, Faber & Faber 2007

Valerie A Reeves & Valerie Showan – Dan Billany, Hull's Lost Hero, Kingston Press 1999

Spurr, Harry A – A Cockney in Arcadia, George Allen & Unwin 1899

Spurr, Harry A – Mel B Spurr, his life, works, writings and recitations, A Brown & Sons 1905

Stevenson, Robert Louis – The Black Arrow, Readers' Digest

www.ingramcontent.com/pod-product-compliance
Lightning Source LLC
Chambersburg PA
CBHW081520040426
42447CB00013B/3284